TEACH YOURSELF DEEP LEARNING IN 24 HOURS

BY

Dr Issa Ngoie

INTRODUCTION TO DEEP LEARNING

What is the difference between AI and ML and DL?

Machine Learning (ML) is commonly used along with AI but it is a subset of AI. ML refers to an AI system that can self-learn based on the algorithm. Systems that get smarter and smarter over time without human intervention is ML. Deep Learning (DL) is a machine learning (ML) applied to large data sets.

Artificial intelligence

Any technique that allows computers to mimic human behavior.

Machine learning

Ability to learn without being explicitly being programmed

Deep learning

Extract pattern from data using neural network.

Traditional programming vs New way of programming a device

Traditional way
Electronic devices = Need to be **programmed**

The new way (Machine learning)= Electronic devices must not be programmed explictly; but **trained** to produce programmed to be used by users for decision making and prediction.

Why training machines?
We are training machines in order for it the help us produce intelligent programs for decision-making and prediction.

So before we usually program machines, but with machine learning we have to train machines

What is machine?

Machine : PC, websites, applications,....

How to train machines?

For training machines we need specific tool or techniques.

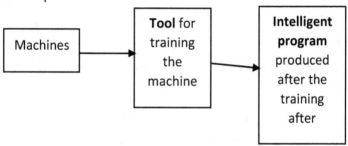

<u>**Types of machine learning tools or techniques for training machines**</u>

We have three tools o techniques:

❖ Supervised learning

- ❖ Unsupervised learning
- ❖ Reinforcement learning

Supervised learning

For training machines, two inputs (X,Y) or features to be used are known or labeled in advance . The job of the supervised tool or algorithm is to find the **relationship** between those two variables or the **mapping** between those two variables.

Input can be: **size(X)** and **color(Y)** example when you want the algorithm to predict the price of a product.

The supervised algorithm will map the relationship between X(size) and Y(Color) ,in order to predict the choice of users or do the prediction on their choices.

X can be considered as = **input**

Y can be considered as = **Output**

Supervised learning algorithms

Various algorithms and **computation techniques** are used in supervised machine learning processes. ...

- ❖ Linear regression. ...
- ❖ Classification
- ❖ Logistic regression. ...
- ❖ Classification
- ❖ Support vector machine (SVM)
- ❖ ......

Linear regression: two inputs X and Y are given, and take continuous numbers such as X=1,2 and Y=3,34

Classification: Inputs or features will have discrete numbers such as : X=1 and Y=0

Logistic regression algorithm : Multiple inputs or features are given, and the goal of the algorithm is to find the mapping.

Example X_n=(X_1=size ,X_2=price, X_3=Weight) and single Y

Sometimes you can have **infinity numbers of inputs**. In this case you have to the support vector machine (SVM) to find the mapping

Typical machine learning algorithms operate by defining set of rules or features in the environment(data),deep learning doing things differently.

In deep learning these features will be learned from the data itself.

For example 1 : when you have a data set ,you will try to look at the age of the population in your data set ,and try to go a bit deeper.

For example, in image processing, lower layers may identify edges, while higher layers may identify the concepts relevant to a human such as digits or letters or faces.

Unsupervised learning

In this techniques, inputs or features are not labelled or known, means sometimes you know X, but not Y. The goal of the algorithm is to find the **structure** in the data.

Below is the list of some popular unsupervised learning algorithms:

❖ K-means clustering.
❖ KNN (k-nearest neighbors)
❖ Hierarchal clustering.
❖ Anomaly detection.
❖ Neural Networks.
❖ Principle Component Analysis.
❖ Independent Component Analysis.

- ❖ Apriori algorithm.

The history of deep learning can be traced back to **1943**, when Walter Pitts and Warren McCulloch created a computer model based on the neural networks of the human brain. They used a combination of algorithms and mathematics they called "threshold logic" to mimic the thought process.

Deep Learning (DL)

In deep learning, algorithms are subset of machine learning or type of machine learning **inspired by the structure of the human brains**.

In deep learning, the structure is **called artificial neural network (ANN)**

So **DL** inspired by the **structure** of human brain, and that structure is called **ANN**, very easy to understand.

Example you need to train a machine in order for it to find the difference between tomatoes (X) and apples (Y) using machine learning.

Let train using machine learning.

In machine learning you have to tell your machines how to differentiate tomatoes and apples by feeding data. These features can be size,...

Let train using deep learning

Using deep learning for finding the difference, the features or inputs will be pick up automatically without human intervention by **neuron networks** without users feed them directly.

Neurons: Core entity of neuron networks, where processing takes place.

So, features or inputs will be feed to neurons, and these neurons are located in the first layer of the networks

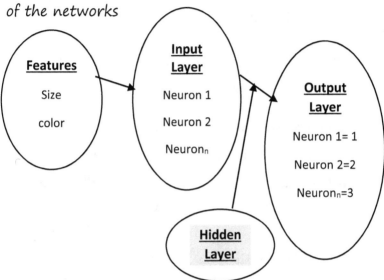

Output layer = Neurons are represented using digits

Between Input layer and Output we have some **hidden layers.**

How information is connected or transferred from one layer to another?

Information is transferred using **connected channel**

The Connection between layers is done via **connected channel.**

Each channel has a value attached to it call **weighted channel** (W), all neurons will have a unique number associated with it called **Bias** (B)

Each Bias(B) must be added to the sum of inputs or features reaching the neurons, and later be send to what we call an **activation function.**

The result of the activated function determine is the neuron is activated, and every activated function is passing information to the following layer.

Bias and **weight** are continually updated or adjusted to produce a well-trained network

Application of deep learning

Customer support: interaction can be done via a robot

Health care

Self-driving cars

Challenges in deep learning

Data: algorithms require a lot of amount of data to train

Computation power: processing a large amount of data requires a **graphical processing unit** (GPU) instead of a CPU. GPU is very expensive and has more cores or thousands of them.

Training time : Deep learning training takes hours or months because of number of layers to be added.

Types of Algorithms used in Deep Learning

- ❖ Convolutional Neural Networks (CNNs)
- ❖ Long Short Term Memory Networks (LSTMs)
- ❖ Recurrent Neural Networks (RNNs)
- ❖ Generative Adversarial Networks (GANs)
- ❖ Radial Basis Function Networks (RBFNs)
- ❖ Multilayer Perceptrons (MLPs)
- ❖ Self Organizing Maps (SOMs)
- ❖ Deep Belief Networks (DBNs)

Three following types of deep neural networks are popularly used today: Multi-Layer Perceptrons (MLP) Convolutional Neural Networks (CNN) Recurrent Neural Networks (RNN)

Neural networks

Neural networks or neural nets, are computing systems inspired by the biological neural networks that constitute animal brains. An ANN is based on a collection of connected units or nodes called artificial neurons, which loosely model the neurons in a biological brain.

Deep learning is a subset of a Machine Learning algorithm that uses multiple layers of neural networks to perform in processing data and computations on a large amount of data. Deep learning algorithm works based on the function and working of the human brain.

Neural networks are **designed to work just like the human brain does**. In the case of recognizing handwriting or facial recognition, the brain very quickly makes some decisions. For example, in the case of facial recognition, the brain might start with "It is female or male? Is it black or white? Is it old or young?

The goal of deep learning is to find features and applied machine learning algorithms on them.

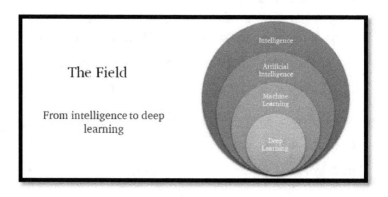

Figure 1

Forward propagation

As the name suggests, the input data is fed in the forward direction through the network. Each hidden layer accepts the input data, processes it as per the activation function and passes to the successive layer.

Why Feed-forward network?

In order to generate some output, the input data should be fed in the forward direction only. The data should not flow in reverse direction during output generation otherwise it would form a cycle and the output could never be generated. Such network configurations are known as **feed-forward network**. The *feed-forward network* helps in *forward propagation*.

At each neuron in a hidden or output layer, the processing happens in two steps:

Preactivation: it is a weighted sum of inputs i.e. the linear transformation of weights w.r.t to inputs available. Based on this aggregated sum and activation function the neuron makes a decision whether to pass this information further or not.

Activation: the calculated weighted sum of inputs is passed to the activation function. An activation function is a mathematical function which adds non-linearity to the network. There are four commonly used and popular activation functions — sigmoid, hyperbolic tangent(tanh), ReLU and Softmax.

What is Neuron?

- **Neurons** (also called neurons or nerve cells) are the fundamental units of the brain and nervous system, the cells responsible for receiving sensory input from the external world, for sending motor commands to our muscles, and for transforming and relaying the electrical signals at every step in between.

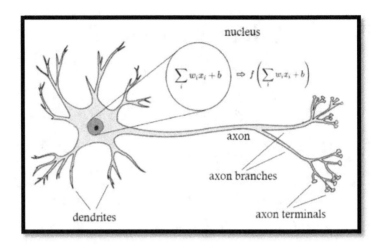

Figure 2: A Biological Neuron

Biological Neuron gets various inputs from "dendrites", then the summation of weights and input is done along with addition bias for each neuron is done in the nucleus.

2. <u>What is the Artificial neural networks (ANN)?</u>

Artificial neural networks are computing systems inspired by the biological neural networks that constitute animal brains.

An ANN is based on a collection of connected units or nodes called artificial neurons, which loosely model the neurons in a biological brain.

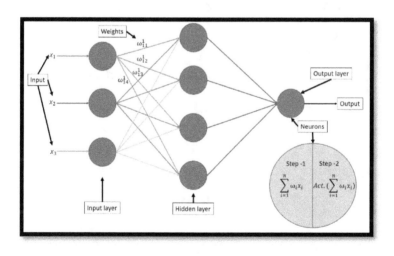

Figure 3 : ANN Overview

From the definition, of neuron and artificial neural network we get to know few terms like input, input layer, weights, Hidden layer, output layer and output.

before that we are defining some **simplifying assumptions:**

Neurons are arranged in layers and layers are arranged sequentially.

Neurons within the same layer do not transfer information with each other.

All data/info enter via the input layer and information/output goes out by the output layer.

All Neurons in layer " l " are connected to all neurons in layer " l+1 ".

Every interconnection in the neural network has a weight associated with it, and every neuron has a bias associated with it.

All Neurons in a particular layer use the same activation function.

— For Demonstration,

I am using a simple neural network for binary classification with three neurons in the input layer and one neuron in the hidden and one neuron in the output layer so my Artificial Neural network looks like this...

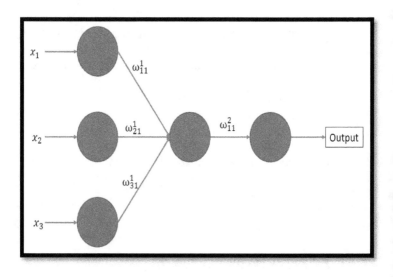

Figure 4: ANN(Binary Classification)

▸ **Number of Neurons:**

Now, You will ask me how you are taking the number of neurons in these layers as three in input and one in hidden and one in output.

- So While defining input layer neurons consider the **number of neurons = number of columns in the dataset.**

- By doing the **Hyperoptimization technique** we will find the number of neurons in hidden layers.

- We need one of the two outputs from **binary classification so one neuron,** If it's a **multiclass classification** we will take, **Number of Neuron = Number of classes in the output layer.**

- **Weight Notations:**

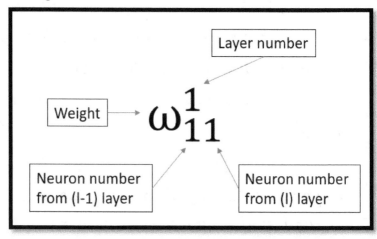

Figure 5: Weight Notation

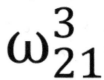

Neuron number 2 from layer 3 is connected to Neuron number 1 from layer 4

Figure 5: Weight connection Understanding

This is how weight notation is normally described...

Recall that models such as linear regression, logistic regressions, SVMs etc. are trained on their coefficients, i.e. the training is to find the optimal values of the coefficient to minimise some cost function.

Neural networks are trained on weights and Biases, which are parameters of the network.

Hyperparameters of ANN or learning algorithm is trained on a fixed set of Hyperparameters- *number of layers, number of neurons in the input layer, hidden and output layers.*

▸ **Neuron Structure:**

From Figure 1: ANN Overview, We have,

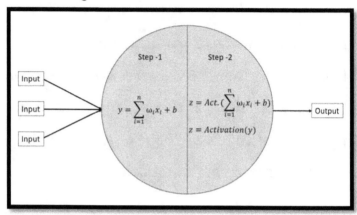

Figure 6: Neuron Structure

Now, From figure 4: ANN,

- We will have three inputs that we will feed to the neuron.

- Step -1, y = Summation of the product of weight and input then the addition of bias to the product of weight and input.

- Then step -2, the value y is fed to the Activation function Which gives the output value(z) of the neuron.

- Similarly, the Information/output value(z) is fed to the next layer neurons as input, Till the output layer.

> ## Activation function:

We are working on a binary classification problem, so for classification, we will use the Sigmoid function.

$$z = \frac{1}{1 + e^{-y}}$$

Where, $y = \omega_1 x_1 + \omega_2 x_2 + \omega_3 x_3 + b$

Figure 7: Sigmoid function

▸ **Loss Function:**

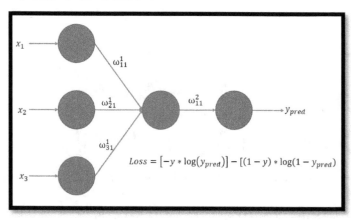

$$Loss = [-y * \log(y_{pred})] - [(1 - y) * \log(1 - y_{pred})]$$

Figure 8: Binary classification error

Loss function in classification, here it is binary cross-entropy.

$$Loss = \left[-y * \log\left(y_{pred}\right)\right] - \left[(1 - y) * \log(1 - y_{pred})\right]$$

For binary classification we have, y = 0 or y = 1.

$$Loss = \begin{cases} -\log(1 - y_{pred}), & \text{if } y = 0 \\ -\log(y_{pred}), & \text{if } y = 1 \end{cases}$$

y_pred is calculated by sigmoid function,

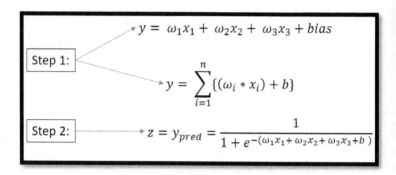

This is the Forward Propagation of the Network.

In Simple terms, Forward propagation means we are moving in only one direction(forward), from input to output in a neural network.

In the next blog, we will get to know the Neural Network training with BackPropagation.

Summary:

1. Calculating, Z =summation[(weights*input)+bias].

2. Choosing Activation function = for binary classification sigmoid function.

3. Substituting the value of " Z ", we will get y_pred.

4. Calculation of Loss using binary cross-entropy.

A Glossary of Neural Network Terms

*O*ne of the greatest road-blocks for newcomers to data science and deep learning is the multitude of terms present on even the most introductory courses. The field has a steep learning curve, as most concepts are intertwined and complementary. To make things worse, most newcomers have little to no machine learning background, making the task even harder. In this article, I break down some of field's most important concepts in a sequential manner, linking each new term to the last.

Let's start with the definition of...

Intelligence: So far, <u>no commonly accepted definition for intelligence exists</u>. The definition is an on-going debate that spans a wide range of fields and disciplines, such as philosophy, psychology, sociology, and computer science. However, although no definition is widely accepted, science has been trying to mimic intelligence for decades, creating...

Artificial Intelligence (AI): The field within Computer Science that studies "intelligent behavior'' in machines. In other words, systems that behave in non-trivially predictable ways. Systems that react and (appear to) reason about themselves and the world around them. This definition is vague as we can't even define intelligence properly. However, something that we can define is learning, which brings us to...

Machine Learning (ML): The task of showing the inputs and outputs of a problem to an algorithm and letting it learn how to solve it. For instance, to create an algorithm that recognizes dogs and cats in pictures by showing it hundreds of photos of pets. Within, ML, a growing approach is:

Deep Learning (DL): The idea of stacking multiple learning algorithms to jointly solve a difficult task. When we are kids, we learn the alphabet, then we learn to read simple words, then full sentences, etc. With practice, we are reading books and forming opinions. In between letters and fluency, several learning steps are involved. In imitation, Deep learning algorithms approach learning by breaking the task down into sequential problems, each one building an increased level of abstraction.

In practice, DL and ML algorithms are frequently the tools of choice for...

Data Science (DS): The study of data, such as acquisition, cleaning, storing, viewing, and processing data. A common misconception is that DL and DS are the same things, as many DS courses feature DL prominently. ML and DL are *tools* for the data scientist, as is SQL, NumPy and, etc.

Data Engineering, Data Analytics, Data Analysis, Cognitive Computing: This area is full of lesser-known synonyms, and confusing terms. Some seem to only exist to sound new and fresh, some make reference to specific tasks within DS. For instance, "analytics" usually refers to exploratory analysis while "engineering" refers to implementing systems for production use. Stick to the widely used terms whenever in doubt, such as "data science".

Artificial Neural Network

(NN): Among several ways of implementing deep learning, neural networks are by far the most popular. In short, they are a stack of simple learning algorithms (called layers) that sequentially process the input, producing an output. This embodies the idea of deep learning by design, as each layer learns a more refined understanding of the input.

Network Layers: All neural networks are made up of layers (as shown in the image above). A layer defines an operation that takes some inputs, some parameters, and produces a set of outputs. For instance, the...

Dense Layer: Is the layer that receives a vector (input) and multiplies it by a matrix (parameters), producing another vector (outputs). While this is one of the most widely used layers in practice, it has a problem, it is:

Linear: Something is linear when it can be decomposed as independent parts, this makes them easy to study. However, a *linear system is no more interesting than the parts that make it.* "A+B" is no more interesting than "A" and "B" themselves. This is opposed by:

Non-Linear: A system is non-linear when its parts are intertwined as a complex whole. A non-linear system cannot be easily factored.

Hence, *the whole is more than the sum of its parts.* For instance, "sine(A + B)" cannot be broken down into "A" terms and "B" terms. Thankfully, any linear system can be made non-linear by means of an...

Activation Function: These are ordinary non-linear functions used in DL that have the sole purpose of receiving input and making it non-linear. In the above example, we made "A + B" non-linear by using the *sine* function. Within DL, the most famous activation function is the:

ReLU: Short of Rectified Linear Unity, defined as ReLU(x) = max(0, x). This is one of the simplest (and most efficient) ways of making something non-linear. That's why it is so popular: it is simple and fast. Combining dense layers and ReLU activations, we can build a...

Dense Network / Fully-Connected Network / Multi-Layer Perceptron: These are all synonyms for the basic neural network: a collection of dense layers interleaved with activation functions. It is important to highlight that, without activation functions, a network would be no more interesting than a single dense layer. The non-linearities are the glue that creates a powerful model out of ordinary parts.

Out of the synonyms for neural networks, one has historical significance...

Perceptron Model: In 1958, Frank Rosenblatt created

a computational model of a neuron: the perceptron, which is the basis for most of what came afterward. Simply put, the perceptron is a weighted sum followed by an activation function. Formally, $P(x; w) = a(x \cdot w)$. This means the perceptron *receives* an "x" vector, *has* a set of weights "w", and *computes* the dot product of "x" with "w" (the weighted sum) and feeds it to "a", the activation function.

Dense Layer (revisited): If an input is fed to many perceptrons at once, as in the figure above, we can simplify the math by "joining" the weights of each perceptron as a matrix, creating

the dense layer:
$D(x; W) = a(x \cdot W)$.
Using this definition, we can build a two-layers network by feeding the result of a dense layer into another, such as:
$D(D(x;W_1);W_2) = a(a(x \cdot W_1) \cdot W_2)$. This showcases an important notion: *neural networks are just math functions.*

In this expression, what we haven't given attention to yet are the...

Weights: Machine learning models define an "operation" that is guided by a set of "weights". By changing a model's weights, we are able to make it do different things. For instance, we might train the same network to recognize cats and dogs or birds and fishes. What changes are the weights, not the network. This brings us to...

them with the expected outputs, and change the weights to make to correct the outputs. The main component of this process is the...

Training: The actual "learning" is performed by the training loop. In simplified terms, training means to feed inputs to a model, collect its outputs, compare

Loss Function: The loss, or error, is a function that measures the "wrongness" of the model. In practice, all we want is to reduce the loss of our models. In other words, we want them to be as correct as possible. To accomplish that, we use a mathematical tool known as...

Gradient Descent: Given a model "M", its weights "θ", the inputs "x", the expected outputs "y" and a loss function "L", we can *optimize* the weights to reduce the loss function by considering the gradient of "L(y, M(x; θ))", known as "∇L". This "∇L" indicates how the loss changes as θ changes. Hence, to reduce the loss we subtract ∇L from θ. This process creates an "improved θ". If we repeat this process over and over, we get...

Epochs: Each time we train our model with every data example we have, we complete an "epoch". Models are typically trained for tens to hundreds of epochs until their losses are reduced to tiny values.

Backpropagation: The above procedure is quite complicated if you are not familiar with the math, yet, I presented a simplified version of it. The complete version is known as backpropagation and has the added complexity that each layer has its own gradient (instead of a single gradient for the whole model, as presented). In this context, some good terms to know are:

SGD / RMSprop / Adam / Nadam / Radam / Ranger /

etc: These are *optimizers*: algorithms that enhance backpropagation to make it faster and better. Understanding these methods is an advanced topic. In practice, everyone uses Adam 95% of the time. Another useful term to know is...

Learning Rate: During training, it works best to update weights in baby steps. While this seems counter-intuitive, it improves convergence. Common values are 0.01, 0.001 and 0.0001. The learning rate is often a parameter of the optimizer. Another common practice during training is to divide it in...

Batches: We often have more data than we can fit in memory or in GPU. Thus, we cannot compute the gradient for all examples we have. Instead, we can compute it for a small subset (a *batch*) and apply it. For instance, a thousand examples can be divided into sixteen batches of 64 elements, yielding sixteen training gradients.